MARSH SIANUDA (VOL.1)

WHERE WORDS COME FROM WITHIN

SUDARSHAN KUMARESAN

To all those who make things happen in life,

the ones who imaginate and think to make it real.

Contents

Contents

Preface

Deep within the pages of wonder,
one may find words that laugh, cry, love, and ponder.
And over the sense of time, one may make it
right or wrong,
but what remains at the end is
the will-power that has grown quite strong.
Poesys indeed they are,
which contain more or less figures of speech,
not just words aren't they, but carry different emotions
which I believe shall make it a far reach.

Preface

Deep within the pages of wonder,
one may find words that laugh, cry, love, and ponder.
And over the sense of time, one may make it
right or wrong,
But what remains at the end is
the will-power that has grown quite strong.
Poems indeed they are,
which through the use of its figures of speech
are just words, [illegible] different emotions
which I [illegible] the [illegible].

Acknowledgements

Thanking all the readers to make it happen. It is not easy for either me or each one of you, however it is indeed an honor and previledge to share some of my views, thoughts and emotions with the world. And this would not have become possible without your support. So blaming all the beloved readers for my success and hoping to get more love and support, so that I shall get an opportunity to shower some of mine, too...

1. LIFE

"What a life we live ,
in an unsatisfactory way.
Sometimes like an electron, while
sometimes like the Hudson Bay.
We crave for higher elevations,
in our own greedy sight.
Hold on ! Ask yourself once,
"Am I doing it right ?"
We bow down to servitude,
and pretermit the actions of prosperity.
After all, we must never deny,
the true cannotation of life lies in our
Ipseity..."

2. ALWAYS REMEMBER

SMILE is an emotion, not a word,
it should be expressed from within,
never be absurd.
Hurt and pain may move around you,
to and fro.
Always remember, let your smile
grow and grow.
Anger, grief and misery may come and go.
Always remember, let your smile
grow and grow.
You are the only leader of your path,
and the only follower of your lead.
Your emotions are a part of your life,
let they not be destroyed by elseone's knife.
Give a reason to your life,
do not reason your life.
Seasons will change, but
the reasons to live will never go.
Always remember, let your smile
grow and grow...

3. THE TRUTH IS ITSELF A LIE

Sometimes, we accord our entire trust,
onto some lives.
But it does not work out,
at the time of a crise.
It makes us feel downcasted,
up until demise.
Excessively cold, intensively dark.
But we cannot deny,
the truth is itself a lie.
Sometimes, we enhance our anxiety
for the past,
and despair the manoeuvre of the future,
until the last.
Roaring and weeping, for the cause of nothing,
it is the right time, to hit the brick with a swinge.
Bidding farewell, when the time is to live;
set-up your wings to fly up high, as
the truth is itself a lie.
Remember the pit that we fall is the same,
the thing is, we all just provide with different names.

Don't you lose hope, or cease to try.

Just believe that

'Something' is alone, but is still alive.

We cannot rely-in, as much as

the truth is itself a lie...

4. IT IS NOT ABOUT HOW FAR WE LIVE OUR LIVES

"In the devil's own luck,"

"life has always cherished in it's craddle.
When there is nothing left with, but muck,
it has always been a saddle.
But never did we realise it's Alchemy;
as it is not how far we live our lives,
it is how deep we enlighten it bright.
The past has left for us it's trace.
The future is primed with it's baffled maze.
But life has always been a rav,
to teach us how to live the present,
with venture and grace;
as it is not how far we live our lives,
it is how deep we enlighen it bright.
The time shall arise,
when people shall realise.
That life has always been with us,

without exceptions,

but we weren't, without expectations.

Live for you, live within you;

as it is not how far we live our lives,

it is how deep we enlighten it bright...

"

5. HOLD YOURSELF

When you turn into a lie,
and blow-up like a bubble.
When you encounter your life,
inevitably saprring with your rebel.
When things do not go as your will,
and you have fallen into a trouble.
Hold yourself tight, but
hold yourself right!
When the days become cold,
and it is freezing your soul.
When darkness reigns over,
craving for more.
When you are trapped in between
the divine and fallen angel,
and you are seeking for the shore.
Hold yourself tight, but
hold yourself right!

6. FEEDING MY NATION

"As a child, I had a dream,"

"of feeding my entire nation.
But, never did I realise,
there would be so much of complications.
An agronomist, or the son of the soil,
as the names go on,
irrespective of leading myself towards the dusk,
I showed them the beautiful dawn.
I ragged myself hard, my physic
and my soul,
for not me, just for their whole.
And made a severe misconception, of
falling into the dark world of expectations.
Just one or two, not many, might it be,
made me realise, my expectations were
not meant for me.
But neither did I give up, nor did I lose hope,
thou always remember

whatever it takes for me,

I shall never end up holding a rope!

Because, I am on my mission,

towards feeding my nation... ”

7. JUST ME

At times, he was fired to flee,
the one who put fire in me.
The future, that I wanted to see,
he was the one who I desired to be.
Let the sound tune-up higher,
of the person who I admire.
Who is he
the one who took me to the highest of the peaks
and brought back from the darkness of the seas ?
He is just me, just me, me.
When the world was killing with voices,
he made a glaive,
when I was left with no choices,
he moulded me alive.
Who is he
the one who taught me,
the time I felt obscured ?
"Guffaw at ones you fear,
reclaim the every single drop of your tear
and never let the time arise,
when you get disappeared
from the wall of your own fame at mere."

He is just me, just me, me.
So, what did make me love myself?
Is he a drow or just a fortunate elf?
For whoever he is, a beast or a being,
nothing matters to me, not even a thing.
As he is me, and I am him,
our affinity has reached the equiibrium,
sometimes, over the brim.
For all the aid he has provided,
I am obliged, to stay united.
Who is he
the one, who turned my life to a comb of honey,
and himself as a bee ?
He is just me, just me, me...

8. THE KNITTER

Underneath the horizon, till the pristine sun shone,
never did I hear any breathe besides me,
but I wasn't alone.
Into the woods, where my own existence lie,
where the delightful blossoms binded by
the iron-willed vines,
were now unshackled, as the sacred breeze passes by.
Each with their beloved ones, just was a moment of surprise,
where there was one for the shoulder, and
the other for the cry.
But I ! I felt none of their fluke, the light,
which the charming blossoms have might.
Wrapped in a buttoned Ramie Magnolia,
tucked inside the antique shredded pyjamas,
had no hens to gaze, no chickens to amaze.
Bounded by myself entirely, I did have a family.
Family, thou think of the cute little drools,
but I think of my very own tools.
Was called an orphan, even with the existence of my gene,
crises hit me with a brick, since I was a teen.
So, I was raised by a Knitter, quite old and pale,
who spent his entire life,

leaving behind beautiful trails.
The Interlock, the Fleece and
the knitted French Terry,
the Fisherman Rib Knit, would each quite vary.
As a Jr.Knitter, I was taught to carve,
the most beautiful outfits of all times,
beginning with the hold of the yarn,
I became his mime.
Before I lived with him but
now, he resides in me.
His teachings are always within me and it is true,
for even if, he is no more a part of the crew.
I am the Knitter, the warden of the garment world,
I protect and preserve the heritage,
for all my inestimable handicrafts,
I furled...

9. FINALLY, WE NEVER BROKE APART

Time, has changed things a lot,
since the trap, in which we two were caught.
I believed in you and you believed in me,
but, 'Oh Fate!' Gave us the roles,
which we weren't supposed to be.
However, we did have a beautiful start,
but finally, we broke apart.
None of us imagined the life,
in the absence of ourselves, would mean.
Was is too early, to ruin our teen ?
Like a mile stone on the road
you'd always guide me,
like the light-house in the storm
you'd always find me.
Untimely, never did we ever depart,
but finally we broke apart.
The moment has now arisen,
to view our lives above the horizon.
For you feel what I do,
let us live a life, which is soulfully true.

Ticking the clock behind would
lead us to sorrow and distress,
let us tick the chronometer
from any further muck and mess.
Just for another Ton-80 shall we
aim our dart,
believe me, finally, we never broke apart...

10. AN OBLIVIOUS SOUL

Cried hard, with an ignorant sight,
thought the loved ones were trespassers
she might.
'Timidly residing inside denailism, she is"
they said,
that even fate, led this poor oblivious soul
confined to death.
The healers, as they are so called,
responded with a gloomy nod.
Nothing could have been done,
atleast not like Mrs.Lucy
her life would have easily returned.
Dada seemed emotionless, filled with silence,
resisting himself, restricting from being carried away,
performed the role he was prepared for.
But Mama, yes she !
The one poured out the tears of dolor and love,
just as the active steam vents,
just as those evergreen who have lost their grove.
As for others, it was just an oblivious soul.

I stood aside, hesitated and clueless,
thought would lose her, before I could confess.
By looking at those cute sparkling eyes, I felt her
inside myself entirly,
the eyes that said, this was not the right time to leave.
Not more than a year did we differ by ages,
I still remember the time I was bedridden like you,
and you medicined on my broken knee,
tying bandages.
Then why now ! Did you leave me all alone,
or did I fail to hear your suffering moan.
For if it is me, the cause for your misery,
it is not you but me, the oblivious soul.
Do you remember of the very incident with Mrs.Lucy,
the puffed, furry cat
who risked for her young ones,
and fought bravely with Douchebag the Rat ?
The true medicine for your sickness is none other than
your words of gold,
the words that would bring you back from
the oblivious soul.
So don't you worry, for if you think I won't be there for you,
the healer said you would soon get together with
the Robinson's crew.
I pray to the Almighty,
to let us stand for each other again.
Just as the chirping parakeets, we shall become a whole,

to enrich our lost lives, the life

without an oblivious soul.

11. I CAN, THEREFORE I WILL

Just as modest as the sun
I persevere from up above,
facing the lightning all by myself, while
let the rest run,
I followed my trace at every crest and trough.
I figured it out to proceed calmly staying still,
and just thought, I can, therefore I will !
At times, situations stun me more than like a taser,
and fill into me some electrons with it's zappy zap,
but wait ! Memories do not get erased easily,
with an eraser
or just by an alien snap.
I kept finding solutions to problems which
never were created, until
when I realised, I can, therefore I will !
Over the years, people fail to learn,
and opt for achieving nothingness,
into oblivion when they turn,
they remember the life that was nothing but
simply a mess.

However, I, in my case, my experience
got myself connected with the puzzle.
And opted some time for the gaps to fill,
not letting my soul fall into the darkness
deep and dense,
I hence decided, I can, therefore I will !

12. THE TRIDENT

I have a trident, nevertheless, the same,
if I tell you as such, you may find me lame.
But yes ! I have got one, which holds the power
of the elementals,
hidden beneath the core of the crust,
it is simply monumental.
My trident indeed, quite differ in model
as much as I remember, obtained it's power
when I was in a cradle.
Swinging around to and fro,
in a sense of curiosity,
I began to feel more soulful and mighty.
Maybe this could have been the beginning
of a new aeon,
where I was the ruler of my own world,
holding the trident which I can move on.
Seventeen years passed, since I have been
engaging with these three divine beings,
the ones I call the 'Trident', the ones with whom
I spread up my wings.
'Beings' the word may have confused you a bit,
but indeed, it is true and not a wit.

The trident of my life, the ones I neve fail to
view at any angle,
always sucked me into the ocean of success, like
the Bermuda Triangle.
The first, I would say, the creator of my very existence,
my beloved family,
followed by the footsteps that led my soul
towards brightness,
my righteous rav.
The final one, neither led nor followed me, but
always stood besides and became a part of me.
At times of sorrow, at times of misery,
they were always there, forming a cavalry.
And gazed at my joyful expression, at times of happiness
and made themselves happy, within,
my merry mates.
The jewels, which I shall never let pass over,
the trident it is, which
I shall hold forever...

13. YOU AND ME

It has been a week or two since
we ever met each other,
but neither did your concern for me, nor did
my solicitude for you, even bother.
Wandering around in search of success, we were,
that we failed to realise the same ultimate goal,
we conferred.
The day one was quite a coincidence
out of nowhere, I did appear,
but it went well than I thought, it would
for a personality as shy as me
we finally made up our minds clear.
I was a bit scared, kind of nervous
at our first conversation,
thought would end up like a war, between
two rival nations.
In the very beginning I made myself well prepared,
but looking at that charming appearance of yours
the only thing I could possibly do is stare.
Thought it would take a year or more to get into you
as an honest mate,
never expected it to happen on the same day and indeed

according to you, it was not too late.
What made me think over you more, is that
we being the only one to share the same interests together,
seemed like we were in the same ship,
facing the stormy weather.
I still remember the time when I proposed a question stating,
"You care about me ?"
Which I really meant and which was true,
I shall never forget the perfecto reply of yours,
"Isn't that the bare minimum of what friends do ?'
You have always been a light of hope to my darkness,
and guided me in life, to avoid any further muck and mess.
For today, we shall be distantly far away,
but the memories we shared, and the care for each other
shall forever stay.
For I have seen you, what you have seen in me too,
where, you are a part of me and
I am a part of you...

14. INCORRECT PERCEPTIONS

Life turns out to be an opaque mirror
bearing more than one unique faces,
the number does vary along with time
with the change of different phases.
But the state of vision of various observations,
always dominate the hold of
incorrect perceptions.
We get approved towards lie, without
acknowledging the essence of reality,
and often fail to judge the situation, rather we
move on towards the personality.
"He looks evil ! Maybe, he is the one to be blamed",
we suppose,
and move an incorrect piece of wisdom
which in turn leads to regression,
without an oppose.
Over and over, we make errors of
virtual intepretations,
and often generate a sense of
incorrect perceptions.

The existence of one's liability towards situations
depend upon one's own direction of approach,
which at personal level, should never be encouraged
to encroach.
Because, it is when we become able to view
things from an unlike perspective or administration,
we gain the immense power of eliminating
incorrect perceptions...

15. ANOTHER LIE

What can you say on your actions, as a whole ?
Let it be the truth that pan out
from your hearted soul.
Beginning with the pristine sun shine, and
ending with the moonlight, all wrapped dark and old,
where the days are quite brighter and the nights
so cold.
Wandering in disguise, we often pose emotions
that make us cry,
but remember ! It is not another way out, just
another lie.
Fallen deep beneath the burden of misery,
awaiting for some divine spirit to lift us up
and set us free.
Weeping under the shade of hope,
we often let go the transcendence of happiness
off the rope.
Upon everything we crave for, just to make it happen
before we die,
we try finding new ways out which is
another lie.
Living to feel, to make it the only one,

the feel which is as powerful as
the UY Scuti Sun.
As an infant, we wonder to turn over
simple to extraordinary,
where our imaginations and thoughts do not
quite vary.
Let it be a new beginning to your life
let it be just another try,
for all that shall transpire from a new seedling
with a new smile,
let it not just be
another lie...

16. THE RISE OF THE FALLEN ERA

"Over the years,
choked with bloodshed and fear.
None imagined freedom,
would have been existed
even at mere.
Over the moonlight, it just happened
without any call, neither an alarm
could one possibly hear.
Violating the pleasant silence of the sky
leaving behind the trace of
several hearts threatened.
Neither one, nor two but dozens,
of innocent souls getting dissipated
for the might of an abominable history.
"The King of Khangas Valleys", rightfully so
as he was called,
pledged upon his life, as the protector for all.
Manifested his entire integrity in the War of the Pacific.
Although a remarkable win, it turned out to be terrific.

Holding the 'Sword of Wisdom', he devoured the
'Ruthless Reed the Pirate'.
Taking in the 'Curse of Daemon' turning himself,
into a gigantic being,
never did he ever return back as the victorious king.
Leaving behind the traumatic end of
the 'Kingdom of Khangas Valleys'
it was the cry of
the soulful buds and several families,
it was the rise of the fallen era...
"

17. GEAR UP

Gear up ! For the time has arrived to chase
in what you fear for,
all the things that have bogged down the pace
and is craving for more.
Gear up ! Because no one can become
what you aspire to ,
aiding others to follow their footsteps,
make your own path through.
Dreaming crazy is not an unforgivable offence,
but making it happen in reality
shall make up more sense.
Gear up ! As it is hard to make sacrifices
for the loved ones,
become ready to rise up before
setting down like the sun.
Innovative minds do not make out quite well at first,
imaginate your ideas to make it real
and to fill up everyone's thirst.
Gear up ! For people believe you cannot
but do you ?
Questioning yourself rather seeking answers
far and wide,

would probably provide a clear view of
the right side.
Gear up ! Because there are a lot of changes to make,
gain more power as there are a lot of responsibilities
to undertake.
Turn things right what others
have proven inaccurate,
for the reason that, there is always a space for trials
where the time is not too late.

18. THE DAWN OF THE CYBER SPHERE

When the world was running with hands,
carving, architecture, moulding, one-too-many.
One could possibly view, at the most feel
the conscientious and diligent breadwinners,
at the finest of sand
working for their beloved ones, to earn
their very first penny.
Love and loyalty, scattered across the widest of sight,
where humans were dependent on humans
turning the wrong into right.
With the world so beautiful and green
from far away, the blue dots connecting each other
could be easily seen.
However, some lost their hope living
carrying out unendurable tasks,
while the others smothered their faces,
concealing their despair and darkness
wearing different masks.
When one fine day, there showed up
a sudden change,

which transformed the lives of various beings,
froma a far range.
'Machines' as they were named so,
turned out to become a boon, for
the entire globe to grow.
Aiding to the human race, it gave rise to
rapid urbanization,
like a super fast express rail, it travelled to various
different nations.
No matter how much, significant these bots
proved to be,
they have always been beaten
down the community.
But looking at the present condition,
having a keen view over the entire situation.
Machines have proved their importance
in the modern world
and imposed a sense of threat and fear
over the past few years,
making it happen of what everyone
feared the most
the dawn of the cyber sphere...

19. THE ODD FROM THE HERD

Being the odd from the herd,
made me feel quite absurd.
Varying from the rest, at every aspect,
calling me upon by all, as the suspect.
They decolourize me with their very own words,
'The Coal of Commonality' is the term
they conferred.
Sharing the common womb, till
fetching up the common tomb.
The time we all at once purred,
I was still termed as 'The Odd From The Herd'.
Thinking all over I realised,
I was just another Aerogel cloud slice !
No more I stated, 'The Coal of Commonality',
only believed to be the coal to fuel-up
Individuality.
Being the odd from the herd did make me peculiar,
and grateful to the Almighty's alchemy,
for bestowing the odds and idiosyncrasy
all upon me...

20. THERE IS A LONG WAY TO GO

At times we break down during crises
to make ourselves better than before,
hitting our heads with the brick we become wild
and desperate to the core.
Thoughts of demise wander around our minds
at times of failure, to and fro,
believing it to be the end, we forget that
there is a long way to go.
A number of times we give up
on our wrong deeds or ways,
what if! We think the right
until our mind stales.
Failures are not considered as pessimistic
or wrong,
but we shall lose completely, if we lack in keeping
our will power strong.
Creating a mess around simplified way of life
which may eventually grow,
we shall never forget
there is a long way to go.

We may not be the 'Captain of My Ship' or
the 'Master of My Sea' today,
but do remember, where there is a will
there is always a way.
People who live for the sake of living
die for nothing,
but those who live to enlighten other souls
remain in every heart, not by parts
but as a whole.
Strive to survive to enrich lives, which
in turn enriches oneself much more,
for there is always a long way to go...

21. WARRIOR

People's insight worry about
the bread and butter needs of their heir,
well I ! I fret about the lives of the people
out there.
Coming out as a super hero, I reside
as an ordinary personality from within,
with a worn veiled attire, pale and thin.
You may think but it isn't true,
that I might have been the roaring thunder just
after the bolt from the blue.
But I was born with flaws and fears,
which indeed turned me out into a warrior.
They said, "You require courage to fight",
which unfortunately I lacked in the most,
was bullied by my fellow mates at all possible
ways one might
I looked upon them as a haunting ghost.
Then what made me become, I always dreamt of ?
What made me turn away, from all the ones I loved ?
Truly it should be the grit I carried along with me
which grew year after year,
which indeed turned me out into a warrior.

Now I look upon myself as a living weapon,
to seek dominance of the good over the evil.
I preserve my responsibility for the rise of
the new era
with all my solidity and will.
However, it took some valuable jewels of my life
which I could never hope to retain,
urging me to start from where it all began
incurred great loss and pain.
Standing in front of my beloved folk, as the knight
in shining armour with the eternal sword carrier,
I was, am and shall always live as a warrior...

22. OH WONDER ! I WONDER

Oh wonder ! I wonder
how could the kite possibly fly ?
With pride and a sight of sore eyes.
Without any hopes of a bridle
and a tail nearby...
Oh wonder ! I wonder
how could the fisch possibly swim
or even take-in the O2, underwater rim ?
In absence of it's flipper or the only gills
could it make it to it's destiny,
just by taking some supplementary pills...
Oh wonder ! I wonder
Could the rivulet ever be able to reach it's objective ?
If there exist any cheerful breeze passing by inactive.
Or could the magnificent boulders ever be able to
stand determined,
if there wasn't any brace of the Mother Earth herself
with her der mund.
Just as the wonders of the Evergreen themselves are
quite reliable on each other to achieve excellence.

We on the other side are just an element
then why that pride and prejudice ?
Why letting oneself towards divergence ?
When a dawdler is meaninglesswithout it's shell,
what if we shower gratitude towards those pure souls
who lifted us towards heaven,
when the head was in the clouds and
fended off with their mushy support,
at the time of our fall and blunder.
Oh wonder ! I wonder...

23. RETURNING HOMELAND

What if I start with the existence of a heavenly site
filled with water so holy and finest of sand ?
you might consider me a maniac, but I am right
it is none other than my jovial homeland.
More than houses it is occupied by the evergreen
and makes one feel more fresh,
connecting with their fellow beings.
Farming is considered as the major occupation there,
where people are always present to shower love and care.
It was during the end of April
when this wonderful opportunity knocked at
the door of mine,
leaving my loved ones behind, quite
downcasted me
but I had to follow the rules, I had to follow
the lines.
I was there for days of fifteen,
and wandered around the wonders with curiosity
and keen.
Although I cam along with no company

lived along with myself, I had no friends
to play with any.
But then I realised that I wasn't alone
and had the greatest green being to play with,
we spent our valuable time, valuing each other
with Nature being my whole and soul friend
it all felt like a myth.
Never will I ever forget the alchemy of this journey
of my life,
leaving behind a sense of sensibility and joy.
I would say it is a dream come true and
shall always expand,
for it enlightened the soul of mine
returning homeland...

24. MIND NOT ME

It's been ages since we met at first,
the time I remember I was craving for thirst.
Nothing else but except you
would have changed my mood,
the mantra you imposed upon me
did help me soothe.
Hoping for a better tomorrow
when I grew up as an adolescent,
my sanity and that soul of mine
waived away the ability of innocence.
Moreover, no lure to think about it there was,
except one from the beginning
of the very cause.
So I startled and rattled
for the cause of my very being.
Could have opted for some gloom-ridden choices
particularly bid farewell,
but I hesitated.
Perceived about the 'You-Me' relationship
the time where it all started,
could have taken some far flung
the memories, that I spotted.

I was within you and you within me,
all were to be felt nothing to see.
For folk who fail to understand about we.
I would say just
mind not me...

25. TO MAMA, WITH LOVE

How can I repay you mama of mine ?
You who moulded with the beautiful hands of yours
and made me sublime.
Led the way of my life, avoiding me
to commit any crime,
moreover, taught me how to live, how to shine.
From the day it all began,
you were always there to hold my hand.
On your lappy cushion when I fell asleep,
you patted on me, so that I dream in deep.
And till the time I was awake,
Neither did you blink a bit, nor did you
take a break.
Sometimes you became my three dimensional shadow,
while at times you turned into a fierce tigress though.
Still I remember me performing
in front of the folks,
and you being the only one giggling and laughing
at my lame jokes.
You were a pillar to my existence and

my everything too,
and also the Captain of the Ship, where
I was a part of the crew.
You displayed this wonderful sight and soul to me,
for which eternally grateful,
I am supposed to be.
In your absence, I might have been
just a grain of sand filled with nothingness,
or just a machine weighing the absence of my own existence
more or less.
For the time shall come, when,
you turn into an infant and myself as your mama,
where I promise to treat you the same
you treated me back then.
Applying the lessons learnt from you,
acknowledging life with a glowing smile
at every crest and trough,
a living poesy from your living soul,
I thereupon write this
to mama with love...

9 798887 046327

Printed by Libri Plureos GmbH in Hamburg,
Germany